World War II
PUZZLE BOOK

GRAB A PENCIL PRESS

CARLISLE, MASSACHUSETTS

World War II Puzzle Book

Copyright © 2016 Applewood Books, Inc.

All rights reserved. No part of this book may be
reproduced in any form or by any electronic or
mechanical means without permission in
writing from the publisher, except by a
reviewer who may quote brief
passages in a review.

ISBN: 978-0-9882885-5-3

Published by
GRAB A PENCIL PRESS
an imprint of Applewood Books
Carlisle, Massachusetts 01741
www.grabapencilpress.com

10 9 8 7 6 5 4 3 2 1

Manufactured in the United States of America

World War II
PUZZLE BOOK

"Yesterday, December 7, 1941, a date that will live in infamy, the United States was suddenly and deliberately attacked by naval and air forces of the Empire of Japan."

President Franklin D. Roosevelt
before the U.S. Congress, December 8, 1941

So began the United States' entry into World War II after fighter planes attacked Pearl Harbor on the island of Oahu, Hawaii. The roots of the war went as far back as the end of World War I, with Germany trying to recover from the costs (reparations) they were forced to pay European neighbors for the destruction left behind. The German people were in an endless cycle of poverty and hopelessness that was compounded by the worldwide depression of the 1930s. In their search for a turnaround, Adolf Hitler's Nazi Party offered hope for a stronger country. This turnaround involved building military strength and expanding into new territories. The tipping point occurred in September 1939 when Germany invaded Poland, causing Britain and France to declare war on Germany after years of trying to maintain peaceful relations. Germany joined with Italy and Japan to form the Axis powers, their purpose being to expand and dominate other countries.The Allied Powers included Britain, France, the Soviet Union, and the United States. Over the course of two years Germans attacked the Netherlands, Belgium, France, Britain, and finally the Soviet Union. The truly worldwide war was fought on other fronts as well, with Italians in Africa and the Mediterranean and the Japanese in the Pacific Ocean region.

This book includes the countries and leaders involved in World War II and covers the conflict from beginning to end. In addition to the major fronts on which the war was fought, in Europe and the Pacific, the role of the United States' home front was key to the Allies achieving victory. The transport and fighting craft on land, air, and sea played key roles in major battles. Breaking the German and Japanese code was an important part of achieving an advantage in fighting. The Allies also used their own codes to stay ahead of the enemy. Jewish concentration camps in Germany and Japanese detainment camps in the United States speak to the horrid consequences of war. World War II resulted in millions of deaths and tremendous destruction and suffering. As the Allies won the war, concluding with atomic bombs dropped in Japan, Europe's political boundaries were reshaped and new alliances formed.

PUZZLE ANSWERS ON BACK PAGES

The Rise of Dictators

ACROSS

4. Eager for a leader to improve the economy, ___ ___ was made dictator of Germany in 1933.

6. The German dictator led the ___ Party in Germany.

9. Germany started World War II as friends with ___ but later invaded this country by surprise.

11. Trying to grow its empire, Japan had taken over big parts of ___ in 1937 before the start of World War II.

12. The United ___ was formed after World War II to try to keep peace.

13. The Treaty of ___ forced Germany to pay for damages from World War I.

15. In 1936 Germany signed the Rome-Berlin Treaty with Italian dictator Benito ___.

16. ___ was U.S. president when World War II began.

DOWN

1. The countries that fought against Germany were part of the ___ powers.

2. Isolating itself from world issues, the ___ ___ stayed out of events leading to World War II.

3. World War II began in September 1939 when Germany invaded ___.

5. In the late 1920s and 1930s the Great ___ ruined world economies.

7. Before World War II began, in 1938 Germany took back ___, a country it controlled in World War I.

8. The first countries to declare war on Germany were Great Britain and ___.

10. When the German leader took power in 1933 he held the title of ___.

14. As Germany began to rearm during the 1930s it joined forces with ___ to its south.

PORTRAITS OF CHURCHILL, ROOSEVELT, AND STALIN BY WILLIAM TIMYM.

Leaders

ACROSS

4. President Roosevelt focused more on domestic than ___ policy before the United States was attacked.

5. The ___ of Japan expanded its territory to gain more power and resources.

6. Joseph Stalin, the dictator of the ___ ___, joined forces with the Allies when Germany turned against him.

7. The 33rd President, Harry ___, ordered bombs be dropped on Japan to force it to surrender.

9. The ___ dictator, Benito Mussolini, formed an alliance with Germany during World War II.

13. General George ___ commanded the Third Army and pushed the Germans back in France.

14. First Lady Eleanor ___ worked for the Red Cross and served the wounded in Europe and the Pacific during the war.

15. Mao Zedong, leader of the ___ Party in China, had little power during World War II because of Japan's control over that part of the world.

16. Free France was led by President Charles ___ from 1944 to 1946.

DOWN

1. The leader of Great Britain during World War II held the title of ___ ___.

2. ___ ___ wrote a diary that dealt with her life while hiding from the Germans.

3. Japan's ___ ordered the bombing of Pearl Harbor in Hawaii.

4. The 32nd President of the U.S., ___ Roosevelt, declared war after the attack on Pearl Harbor.

8. The commander of the Allied forces in the Pacific was General Douglas ___.

10. Army five-star general and future U.S. president Dwight ___ led Allied forces in Europe.

11. German Chancellor ___ led the Nazi Party and sought more territory in taking over European countries.

12. Prime Minister ___ of Great Britain stood up to the Germans in leading the Allied countries.

Transport

ACROSS

2. The German air force, called the ___, played a large role in controlling Western Europe early in the war.

5. The heavy tank used by the Germans in the war was called the ___ II.

6. An aircraft that descended directly toward its target before dropping its bomb was called a ___ ___.

7. Warships traveling in groups formed a ___ to be protected from German submarine attacks.

10. ___ was the name of the manufacturer of most of the fighter aircraft used by the Germans.

11. The M4 ___ tank was the ground vehicle used most by United States and Allied forces in Europe.

13. Mitsubishi A6M ___ was a long-range fighter aircraft used by the Japanese.

14. The ___ ___ was the aircraft that dropped the atomic bombs on Hiroshima and Nagasaki.

DOWN

1. Japanese pilots who flew their fighter planes into enemy warships on purpose were called ___.

3. German submarines, called ___, patrolled the Atlantic Ocean in the hundreds during the War.

4. The U.S.-made B-17 ___ ___ was a heavy bomber flown during World War II.

8. The P-51 ___ was a single-seat fighter bomber built by the U.S. for use in World War II and the Korean War.

9. The biggest loss at Pearl Harbor was when 1,100 troops were lost with the sinking of the ___ ___ .

12. The aircraft carriers *Enterprise, Yorktown,* and *Hornet* were involved in the Battle of ___ .

Sudoku

Solving a sudoku puzzle can be rather tricky, but the rules of the game are quite simple.

A sudoku puzzle is a grid of squares or cells. The objective of these sudoku is for each row and column to have all the letters that spell the word at the top of the puzzle. But, you must enter a letter in each cell in such a way that each horizontal row contains each letter only once and each vertical column contains each letter only once.

ARMY

	A	M	
R			Y
		R	

NAVY

			Y
		N	
			A
A	V		

CORPSMEN

	C		E	O	S		
	N					C	P
C						M	
		O	M		C		
	R	S		E			
M					P		R
	M		C			P	E
		P				S	

WAR BONDS

W		A		O	D		
	R			B			N
		N				B	W
		S	O		A		
			A		N	S	R
R	S						
		R	W	D		O	
S	O			N	R		

HITLER

H				T	L
		E			
	T	L	R		
	R			L	
L					I
		I		E	T

TRUMAN

	T			R	
	U			T	
T	N	U		A	R
A	R	M			T
	M			N	
	A			M	

HARRY S. TRUMAN BY GRETA KEMPLER

Code Breaking

Morse code was a vital means of Allied communication during World War II. It was used by warships and aircraft to communicate with their bases. Armies on the move needed code communicated by radio because telegraph and telephone lines could not be built fast enough. On ships, voice radio messages were limited in their range and security. Messages in code were easier to send and provided more security. The dots and dashes below represent the letters of the Morse alphabet.

A = • —	J = • — — —	S = • • •
B = — • • •	K = — • —	T = —
C = — • — •	L = • — • •	U = • • —
D = — • •	M = — —	V = • • • —
E = •	N = — •	W = • — —
F = • • — •	O = — — —	X = — • • —
G = — — •	P = • — — •	Y = — • — —
H = • • • •	Q = — — • —	Z = — — • •
I = • •	R = • — •	

Fill in the proper answer below by decoding the Morse letters.

The Germans used an __ENIGMA__ machine in an effort to code and decode

messages. The Allies were able to crack the code. A code that the Germans were not able

to break was the language of the Native American __NAVAJO__ tribe.

Some early electronic __COMPUTERS__ aided in breaking the

German code. Spies and secret agents were used by both sides during the war. The British

were able to track down German spies and turn them into double agents for Great Britain

in what was called the __DOUBLE__ __CROSS__

system. While the U.S. spy agency, the Office of Strategic Services, hired Germans to

become spies to find out about German attack plans, the German spy agency, named

__ABWEHR__ , was ignored by those high up in the Nazi Party, making it

ineffective. A new technology that was first used by the British to detect German aircraft

was __RADAR__ . The largest advance in naval technology was the use of

__AIRCRAFT__ __CARRIERS__ , which

provided for air attacks anywhere in the ocean.

We Can Do It!

J. HOWARD MILLER FOR WESTINGHOUSE ELECTRIC.

11. New York Yankee baseball player Joe ___ enlisted and fought in the war.

13. Japanese-Americans were moved to ___ camps.

15. The president told the commissioner of ___ to continue playing games to keep up public morale.

DOWN

1. The United States entered World War II when Japan attacked ___ ___ .

2. Rationing in the U.S. included nylon used in making __ for airborne military troops.

3. ___ was rationed, making transport more difficult, in addition to sugar, meat, butter, and coal.

On the U.S. Home Front

ACROSS

4. The Native American ___ tribe's language was used as a secret code against the Germans during the war.

6. Some 80,000 ___ were manufactured in the U.S. for use in ground battles in Europe.

7. The pointing finger of ___ ___ *'I Want You For U.S. Army'* poster, originally designed in 1917, during WWI, was used extensively to recruit soldiers during WWII as well.

8. Women who worked in factories building military fighting vehicles were given the name ___ the ___ .

5. The __ __ grew from 190,000 servicemen to 10 million by war's end in 1945.

9. In 1942 a rationing program was begun whereby meat, butter, and other necessities were paid for by ___ .

10. About 40 percent of all vegetables raised in the U.S. during the war were grown in ___ gardens.

12. To help in the funding of the war, celebrities including Bob Hope promoted war ___ .

13. President Roosevelt said before Congress that the Japanese attack on Hawaii was a day that would live in __ .

14. All ___ scripts during the war had to be approved by the government.

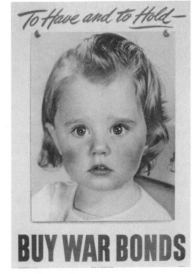

To Have and to Hold—

BUY WAR BONDS

The War in Europe

ACROSS

4. A major defeat for Germany occurred in the southern Soviet Union at the Battle of ___ .

6. The hard-fought D-Day invasion in France took place at ___ Beach.

8. The Battle of ___ was an effort by Germany to destroy the Royal Air Force.

9. The United States, France, and Britain made up the ___ forces in the European war.

11. After the Allies won back France, in Belgium the Battle of the ___ was long but another defeat for Germany.

12. The tactic used by German submarines by surrounding several Allied supply ships at one time was called ___ ___ .

13. The D-Day invasion by British and American forces took place in ___ , France.

DOWN

1. Germany stopped bombing England so fighters could attack ___ .

2. The Third Army of General George ___ supplied extra forces in a key battle in Belgium.

3. Hitler focused attacks on ___ , England, after failing to defeat Great Britain quickly.

5. The Battle of the ___ was Germany's effort to stop supplies from reaching Britain and the Soviet Union.

7. The first wave of attack in France on D-Day was ___ jumping from aircraft.

8. A German defeat and the death of Adolf Hitler took place at the Battle of ___.

10. Hitler's invasion of Britain was called Operation ___ ___.

11. The bombing of Britain was known as the ___ and lasted 57 nights.

The War in the Pacific

ACROSS

2. The Soviet Union attacked Japan in ___ in August 1945, the same month the U.S. dropped atomic bombs on Japanese cities.

4. The Medal of ___ was awarded to 27 Americans for their bravery at Iwo Jima.

5. The U.S. flag was planted on the top of Mount ___ after winning the battle at Iwo Jima.

6. Admiral ___ led the U.S. forces at the Battle of Midway in the Pacific.

8. Three battleships, the U.S.S. *Arizona,* U.S.S. *Utah,* and the U.S.S. ___ were destroyed in the attack on Pearl Harbor.

10. The code name for the beginning invasion by U.S. troops on Guadalcanal was Operation ___ .

12. The U.S. ___ were first to land on Iwo Jima to battle the Japanese.

13. General Douglas ___ commanded the Allied forces in the Pacific.

fused to surrender, even after his troops were forced back to Japan.

DOWN

1. ___, an island in the southwest Pacific, was the first place the U.S. went on the attack against Japan.

2. The U.S.S. ___ provided gun support as Marines began the U.S. invasion of Iwo Jima, Japan.

3. In August 1945 the U.S. dropped atomic bombs on ___ and Nagasaki, Japan.

4. Japanese emperor ___ re-

7. Of the three aircraft carriers involved in the Battle of Midway, only the U.S.S. ___ was sunk.

9. ___-made weapons, aircraft, and vehicles were used in all Pacific War battles.

11. The ___ death march, in which many U.S. and Filipino troops died after capture by the Japanese, took place in the Philippines.

Definition Match

1. Germany's name for the war with the Soviet Union.

2. The date that U.S. and British forces invaded Germans in France.

3. The police force of the Nazi Party in Germany.

4. The powers that included Britain, France, and the United States.

5. The National Socialist German Workers Party name.

6. The name of the program in which scientists created the atomic bomb.

7. The powers that included Germany, Italy, and Japan.

8. The type of government in Germany and Italy that was ruled by dictators.

9. The murder of more than six million Jewish people under Adc Hitler.

10. May 8, 1945, was the date in which victory in Europe was celebrated.

____ a. Gestapo

____ b. Axis

____ c. Holocaust

____ d. D-Day

____ e. V-E Day

____ f. Nazi

____ g. Eastern Front

____ h. Manhattan Project

____ i. Allied

____ j. Fascism

Names and Places of WWII

```
U  B  E  R  L  I  N  D  I  L  B  E  V  I  N  E
R  M  A  O  T  U  T  E  Y  W  E  T  U  H  O  S
O  E  Y  L  A  T  I  G  D  A  O  H  O  C  T  T
B  R  I  E  D  T  R  A  N  S  N  J  D  A  T  A
R  A  M  S  R  I  P  U  A  H  E  A  I  R  A  L
A  C  L  P  E  C  O  L  M  O  T  D  N  M  P  I
H  H  O  E  A  N  O  L  R  R  U  I  O  E  A  N
L  U  T  U  S  R  H  E  O  B  A  T  A  A  N  M
R  R  N  T  A  T  I  O  N  R  B  R  N  C  I  H
A  C  R  A  E  E  R  S  W  O  U  L  E  D  T  I
E  H  C  O  M  D  N  S  H  E  G  I  W  O  S  T
P  I  H  N  T  U  E  I  T  B  R  A  H  U  N  L
A  L  U  E  L  G  R  H  P  T  Y  P  I  G  A  E
R  L  A  D  O  R  S  T  I  N  E  U  D  U  P  R
T  U  N  I  N  I  L  O  S  S  U  M  N  E  A  U
S  M  S  T  A  L  I  N  G  R  A  D  I  A  J  A
```

GENERAL GEORGE S. PATTON

Find the following:

- STALIN
- EISENHOWER
- HITLER
- STALINGRAD
- CHURCHILL
- DEGAULLE
- NORMANDY
- MIDWAY
- PATTON
- MUSSOLINI
- BERLIN
- BATAAN
- PEARL HARBOR
- PARIS
- JAPAN
- ITALY
- TRUMAN
- IWO JIMA

LIBRARY OF CONGRESS, PRINTS & PHOTOGRAPHS DIVISION
TONI FRISSELL COLLECTION, LC-F9-02-4503-320-02

Facts and Trivia

ACROSS

2. The bombs dropped on Hiroshima and Nagasaki were nicknamed "Little Boy" and ___ ___.

4. Operation ___ was another name for the D-Day attack by Allied forces in France.

6. The killing of millions of Jewish people was termed the final ___.

7. Women's Air Force Service Pilots, known as ___, flew planes between army bases and flew cargo planes.

10. President ___ signed a bill in 1988 that paid $20,000 to each survivor of Japanese internment camps during the war.

12. The Japanese dug 11 miles of ___ on the island of Iwo Jima.

DOWN

1. The ___ Project was the code name for secret scientific work to develop the atomic bomb.

2. During his ___ chats while the U.S. was at war, President Roosevelt asked Americans to listen with world maps so that troops could be located.

3. Tokyo ___ was the radio voice of a Japanese woman telling U.S. troops they couldn't win the war.

5. The first group of African-American pilots in World War II was called the ___ airmen.

6. Fake fence ___ were one of the ways in which secret messages were passed between agents during World War II.

8. Soviet leader Joseph ___'s name was combined from the Russian word for *steel* and former leader Vladimir Lenin's name.

9. "Old Blood and Guts" was the nickname given General George ___.

11. Japanese-Americans sent to relocation camps were required to fill out ___ questionnaires.

WOMEN'S AIR FORCE SERVICE PILOTS LOGO

The War's End

ACROSS

3. The ___ Plan, was an American effort and named for the Secretary of State, to provide aid to Western Europe following the end of the War.

4. On October 24, 1945, the Allied countries formed the United ___ in an effort to prevent future world wars.

7. On May 7, 1945, Germany surrendered to the Allies in what was called "Victory in Europe," or ___.

8. Adolf Hitler committed ___ at the end of the war in Europe.

10. Following the war's end, civil war continued in ___ between Communists and nationalists.

12. Western Europe and the United States formed the ___ alliance to fight Communism after World War II.

13. The Allied countries controlled ___ until it regained independence in 1952.

15. On September 2, 1945, Emperor Hirohito and Japan surrendered to General Douglas ___.

DOWN

1. The ___ Pact was created by the Soviet Union and the countries it controlled under Communism following the end of the war.

2. The U.S.S.R. took control of ___ European countries following the war.

5. Germany was split into two countries, with the Allies controlling the western half and the ___ controlling East Germany.

6. A formal apology was made by President George H. W. ___ in 1989 for those Japanese-Americans put in isolation camps during the war.

9. German and Japanese heads of state were brought to trial for violating the rules of war as stated in the ___ Convention.

10. Following the war an arms race known as the ___ War was started between the Soviet Union and U.S. and European countries.

11. War crime trials against 23 powerful Nazi leaders were held in the German city of ___.

14. Roosevelt, Churchill, and Stalin met at the ___ Conference in February 1945 to determine how postwar Europe would be organized.

The Rise of Dictators

```
        A       U   P
        L       N   O
A D O L F■H I T L E R
    E   I       T   A
    P   E   E   E   N A Z I
    R   D   D   D   D
    E           ■       A       F
R U S S I A         S       A U   R
    S       C       T       U S   A
    I   C H I N A   T   N A T I O N S
    O   A           T       R   C
    N   N   V E R S A I L L E S
        C       S       A
        E           I
M U S S O L I N I   T
        L           A
    R O O S E V E L T
        R           Y
```

Leaders

```
            P                           A
            R                           N
    H       I           F O R E I G N   N
    I   E M P E R O R   R               E
    R       E           A           ■   F
S O V I E T ■ U N I O N K               R
    H       M           L               A
    I       I           L   I T A L I A N
    T R U M A N         I               K
    O       A   I       N
            C   S   E       H
C   P A T T O N     I       I
H   R       E   S   R O O S E V E L T
U   R       T   S   N       E
R   H   R O O S E V E L T
C O M M U N I S T   N       O
H   H       R       H       W
I   L               L       E
L       D E G A U L L E     R
L
```

Transport

```
                K
L U F T W A F F E
B           L   A
O           Y   M
A           I   T I G E R
T           N   K
S           G   A
    D I V E■B O M B E R
            F
        C O N V O Y   M
        R           U
    U   T           U
    S   E           S
M E S S E R S C H M I T T
    ■   E           A
    A   S H E R M A N
    R   S           I
    I           D   G
    Z E R O     W
    O           W
E N O L A■G A Y
    A
```

Sudoku

W	N	A	B	O	D	R	S
D	R	O	S	B	W	A	N
A	D	N	R	S	O	B	W
B	W	S	O	R	A	N	D
O	B	D	A	W	N	S	R
R	S	W	N	A	B	D	O
N	A	R	W	D	S	O	B
S	O	B	D	N	R	W	A

TRUMAN

N	T	A	U	R	M
M	U	R	A	T	N
T	N	U	M	A	R
A	R	M	N	U	T
U	M	T	R	N	A
R	A	N	T	M	U

CORPSMEN

P	C	M	E	O	S	R	N
O	N	R	S	M	E	C	P
C	S	E	N	P	R	M	O
R	P	O	M	N	C	E	S
N	R	S	P	E	M	O	C
M	E	C	O	S	P	N	R
S	M	N	C	R	O	P	E
E	O	P	R	C	N	S	M

HITLER

H	I	R	E	T	L
T	L	E	I	H	R
E	T	L	R	I	H
I	R	H	T	L	E
L	E	T	H	R	I
R	H	I	L	E	T

Code Breaking

Enigma
Navajo
computers
Double Cross
Abwehr
radar
aircraft carriers

ARMY

Y	A	M	R
R	M	A	Y
M	R	Y	A
A	Y	R	M

NAVY

V	A	N	Y
Y	N	A	V
N	Y	V	A
A	V	Y	N

On the U.S. Home Front

The War in Europe

The War in the Pacific

Definition Match

1 = g
2 = d
3 = a
4 = i
5 = f
6 = h
7 = b
8 = j
9 = c
10 = e

Names and Places of WWII

```
U B E R L I N D I L B E V I N E
R M A O T U T E Y W E T U H O S
O E Y L A T I G D A O H O C T T
B R I E D T R A N S N J D A T A
R A M S R I P U A H E A I R A L
A C L P E C O L M O T D N M P I
H H O E A N O L R R U I O E A N
L U T U S R H E O B A T A A N M
R R N T A T I O N R B R N C I H
A C R A E E R S W O U L E D T I
E H C O M D N S H E G I W O S T
P I H N T U E I T B R A H U N L
A L U E L G R H P T Y P I G A E
R L A D O R S T I N E U D U P R
T U N I N I L O S S U M N E A U
S M S T A L I N G R A D I A J A
```

Facts and Trivia

```
                              M
              F A T ■ M A N
        R       I           N
        O V E R L O R D      H
        S       E            A
        E     T S            T
          S O L U T I O N     T
          P     S D       W A S P S
          I K E     E     N       T
          K     E           A
          E     G     P     L
          S   R E A G A N   O     I
          E     T     T     Y     N
                T     O           A
          T U N N E L S           L S
                      T           Y
```

The War's End

```
                W       E
              M A R S H A L L
    N A T I O N S       R     S
    B         O         S     T
    B         V E D A Y       E
    U         I         W     R
    S U I C I D E               N
    H         T
        G     U ■
        E     U     C H I N A
        N     N A T O       U
        E     I     L       R
        V     O     D       E
      J A P A N             M
            Y              B
          M A C A R T H U R  R
            L                G
            T
            A
```

TITLES FROM
GRAB A PENCIL PRESS

Abraham Lincoln Crossword Puzzles
American Flag Puzzle Book
American Revolution Crossword Puzzles
Architecture Crossword Puzzles *Volume 1*
Art History Puzzle Book
Benjamin Franklin Puzzle Book
Civil War History Crossword Puzzles
Ellis Island and the Statue of Liberty Crossword Puzzles
George Washington Crossword Puzzles
John Fitzgerald Kennedy Crossword Puzzles
Natural History Activity Book
New York City Crossword Puzzles
Presidents of the United States Crossword Puzzles *Volume 1*
Texas History Crossword Puzzles
Washington, D.C., Puzzle Book *Volume 1*
World War II Puzzle Book
Yellowstone National Park Puzzle Book

COMING SOON
First Ladies Crossword Puzzles
National Parks Puzzle Book
World War II European Theater Puzzle Book
World War II Pacific Theater Puzzle Book

an imprint of Applewood Books
Carlisle, Massachusetts 01741
www.grabapencilpress.com
800.277.5312